Dysfunctional Disciple

By
Larry Forsyth

ISBN: 9-798-5273188-6-9

Table of Contents

Introduction

The purpose of this book is to show how easy it is to love on others and disciple. Jesus called the dysfunctional. He wants the broken and those of us that need work. It is because of his love for us that Jesus wants us to become his followers. When we are broken, dysfunctional, and have hit bottom, we are ready to be transformed into a new being in Jesus Christ.

The word apostle means one who is sent out. When Jesus called the original 12 disciples to follow him, he did not leave the option to go and prepare. He said, "Follow me," and these original men followed him. The twelve disciples were sent out with the following instructions:

> *Do not go among the Gentiles or enter any town of the Samaritans. Go rather to the lost sheep of Israel. As you go, proclaim this message: 'The kingdom of heaven has come near.' Heal the sick, raise the dead, cleanse those who have leprosy, drive out demons. Freely you have received; freely give. Do not get any gold or silver or copper to take with you in your belts— no bag for the journey or extra shirt or sandals or a staff, for the worker is worth his keep. Whatever town or village you enter, search there for some*

worthy person and stay at their house until you leave. As you enter the home, give it your greeting. If the home is deserving, let your peace rest on it; if it is not, let your peace return to you. If anyone will not welcome you or listen to your words, leave that home or town and shake the dust off your feet. Truly, I say to you, it will be more bearable on the day of judgment for the land of Sodom and Gomorrah than for that town. **Matthew 10:5-14**

Jesus instructed his disciples not to take anything with them but the bare essentials. They were to accept hospitality if presented, and if rejected, they were to shake the dust from their feet as a testimony against the town. Jesus knew that it was going to be dangerous for his disciples. He warned them and sent them out with this message:

I am sending you out like sheep among wolves. Therefore be as shrewd as snakes and as innocent as doves. Be on your guard; you will be handed over to the local councils and be flogged in the synagogues. On my account you will be brought before governors and kings as witnesses to them and to the Gentiles. But when they arrest you, do not worry about what to say or how to say it. At that time you will be given what to say, for it will not be you speaking, but the Spirit of your Father speaking through you. **Matthew 10:16-20**

Why is it we find it so hard to just pick up and follow God? Why is it so hard for us to step out of our comfort zones and do as God directs? As we go through each disciple and examine their lives, we will see what made these people dysfunctional disciples. The dictionary defines dysfunctional as not operating normally or properly.

As we delve into the disciples' lives, we will see that they are transformed and changed the minute they meet Jesus. We will see what problems these disciples had and will continue to have to work through as they follow Jesus. The disciples were far from perfect people. Their talents were workers, fishermen, tax collectors, and bosses. They showed us that the standard social behavior for that time and the typical social behavior for the current times cause us to be thought of as dysfunctional. You see, non-Christians see Christians as dysfunctional, and they do not understand why we act as we do. Just as we wonder why the secular people behave as they do, I would suppose. As we delve into these dysfunctional people, we need to examine our lives to see how we are similar but yet different. What are our dysfunctions and how can God use our dysfunction to help others draw closer to him? We are called in the great commission to make disciples of all people and all nations. In the USA, we have gone so far away from Christ that it is now time to make disciples here at home. This is our new mission field. If we do not start standing up, we will lose our religious freedoms. When the pilgrims came here from Europe, it was to escape the religious persecutions of that time. It seems like we have come full circle. Why is it that free nations have a desire to become enslaved?

As we delve into the disciples, lets relate them to ourselves. Let's look at how Jesus used these dysfunctional people of that time and be open to how God can use us now in these times.

❧ Notes: ❧

For Further Examination

The word for Disciple in the Greek language is mathetes, meaning "learner or follower." This word means accepting and following the views and practices of a teacher, in our case, Jesus.

Jesus, during the periods of his ministry, had a lot of followers. He sent out 72 disciples, but he only chose 12.

*After this the Lord appointed seventy-two others and sent them two by two ahead of him to every town and place where he was about to go. **Luke 10:1***

The following is the list of disciples that he specifically chose and commissioned.

*When morning came, he called his disciples to him and chose twelve of them, whom he also designated apostles: Simon (whom he named Peter), his brother Andrew, James, John, Philip, Bartholomew, Matthew, Thomas, James son of Alphaeus, Simon who was called the Zealot, Judas son of James, and Judas Iscariot, who became a traitor. **Luke 6:13-16***

The disciples were also called apostles. The Greek word for apostles is "apostolos" which means one who is sent out with a special commission as a fully authorized representative of the sender, like an ambassador.

❧ Notes: ❧

For Further Examination

Only in the New Testament of the Bible can you find information about the twelve disciples' lives. Throughout the Bible, there have been many men who have chosen to follow and serve God to accomplish his divine plans. Yet these twelve men were selected explicitly by Jesus, chosen to travel with Him. The responsibility of following Jesus was like a heavy ball and chain attached to them. They realized that they would represent Jesus and represent Him long after his death on the cross and his ascension into Heaven. The Disciples' dedication impacted the Church long after their deaths.

So why did Jesus only choose 12 men? In the Bible, numbers are very important. Like the numbers three, seven, and twelve, these numbers frequently suggested completeness and perfection. In the Old Testament, the number twelve represented all of Israel.

All these are the twelve tribes of Israel, and this is what their father said to them when he blessed them, giving each the blessing appropriate to him. **Genesis 49:28**

Further mentions are also found in Joshua 13-19. The Book of Revelation also provides numerous references to the number 12.

12 tribes of Israel

From the tribe of Judah, 12,000 were sealed,

from the tribe of Reuben 12,000,

from the tribe of Gad 12,000,

from the tribe of Asher 12,000,

from the tribe of Naphtali 12,000,

from the tribe of Manasseh 12,000,

from the tribe of Simeon 12,000,

from the tribe of Levi 12,000,

from the tribe of Issachar 12,000,

from the tribe of Zebulun 12,000,

from the tribe of Joseph 12,000,

from the tribe of Benjamin 12,000. **Revelation 7:5-8**

It had a great, high wall with twelve gates, and with twelve angels at the gates. On the gates were written the names of the twelve tribes of Israel. **Revelation 21:12**

✤ Notes: ✤

For Further Examination

12 stars in the woman's crown which symbolizes the 12 sons of Jacob

A great sign appeared in heaven: a woman clothed with the sun, with the moon under her feet and a crown of twelve stars on her head. **Revelation 12:1**

Then he had another dream, and he told it to his brothers. "Listen," he said, "I had another dream, and this time the sun and moon and eleven stars were bowing down to me." **Genesis 37:9**

12 gates of the great high wall of New Jerusalem and 12 angels guarding the heavenly gates

*Therefore rejoice, you heavens
and you who dwell in them!
But woe to the earth and the sea,
because the devil has gone down to you!
He is filled with fury,
because he knows that his time is short.*
Revelation 12:12

12 apostles of the Lamb, which is part of the Church and the body of Christ

The woman was given the two wings of a great eagle, so that she might fly to the place prepared for her in the

wilderness, where she would be taken care of for a time, times and half a time, out of the serpent's reach.
Revelation 12:14

12 pearls or precision stones of different colors adorning the 12 foundations

The wall of the city had twelve foundations, and on them were the names of the twelve apostles of the Lamb.
Revelation 21:14

After this I heard what sounded like the roar of a great multitude in heaven shouting:

"Hallelujah! Salvation and glory and power belong to our God, for true and just are his judgments.

He has condemned the great prostitute who corrupted the earth by her adulteries.

He has avenged on her the blood of his servants." And again they shouted: "Hallelujah! The smoke from her goes up for ever and ever."

The twenty-four elders and the four living creatures fell down and worshiped God, who was seated on the throne. And they cried: "Amen, Hallelujah!" Then a voice came from the throne, saying:

"Praise our God, all you his servants, you who fear him, both great and small!" Then I heard what sounded like a great multitude, like the roar of rushing waters and like loud peals of thunder, shouting: "Hallelujah! For our

Lord God Almighty reigns. Let us rejoice and be glad and give him glory! For the wedding of the Lamb has come, and his bride has made herself ready. Fine linen, bright and clean, was given her to wear." (Fine linen stands for the righteous acts of God's holy people.)

Then the angel said to me, "Write this: Blessed are those who are invited to the wedding supper of the Lamb!" And he added, "These are the true words of God."

At this I fell at his feet to worship him. But he said to me, "Don't do that! I am a fellow servant with you and with your brothers and sisters who hold to the testimony of Jesus. Worship God! For it is the Spirit of prophecy who bears testimony to Jesus." I saw heaven standing open and there before me was a white horse, whose rider is called Faithful and True. With justice he judges and wages war. His eyes are like blazing fire, and on his head are many crowns. He has a name written on him that no one knows but he himself. He is dressed in a robe dipped in blood, and his name is the Word of God. The armies of heaven were following him, riding on white horses and dressed in fine linen, white and clean. Coming out of his mouth is a sharp sword with which to strike down the nations. "He will rule them with an iron scepter." He treads the winepress of the fury of the wrath of God Almighty. On his robe and on his thigh he has this name written:

And I saw an angel standing in the sun, who cried in a loud voice to all the birds flying in midair, "Come, gather together for the great supper of God, so that you may eat

11

the flesh of kings, generals, and the mighty, of horses and their riders, and the flesh of all people, free and slave, great and small."

Then I saw the beast and the kings of the earth and their armies gathered together to wage war against the rider on the horse and his army. But the beast was captured, and with it the false prophet who had performed the signs on its behalf. With these signs he had deluded those who had received the mark of the beast and worshiped its image. The two of them were thrown alive into the fiery lake of burning sulfur. The rest were killed with the sword coming out of the mouth of the rider on the horse, and all the birds gorged themselves on their flesh.

And I saw an angel coming down out of heaven, having the key to the Abyss and holding in his hand a great chain. He seized the dragon, that ancient serpent, who is the devil, or Satan, and bound him for a thousand years. He threw him into the Abyss, and locked and sealed it over him, to keep him from deceiving the nations anymore until the thousand years were ended. After that, he must be set free for a short time.

I saw thrones on which were seated those who had been given authority to judge. And I saw the souls of those who had been beheaded because of their testimony about Jesus and because of the word of God. They had not worshiped the beast or its image and had not received its mark on their foreheads or their hands. They came to life and reigned with Christ a thousand years. (The rest of the dead

*did not come to life until the thousand years were ended.)
This is the first resurrection. Blessed and holy are those
who share in the first resurrection. The second death has
no power over them, but they will be priests of God and of
Christ and will reign with him for a thousand years.*

*When the thousand years are over, Satan will be released
from his prison and will go out to deceive the nations in
the four corners of the earth—Gog and Magog—and to
gather them for battle. In number they are like the sand
on the seashore. They marched across the breadth of the
earth and surrounded the camp of God's people, the city he
loves. But fire came down from heaven and devoured
them. And the devil, who deceived them, was thrown into
the lake of burning sulfur, where the beast and the false
prophet had been thrown. They will be tormented day
and night for ever and ever.*

*Then I saw a great white throne and him who was seated
on it. The earth and the heavens fled from his presence,
and there was no place for them. And I saw the dead, great
and small, standing before the throne, and books were
opened. Another book was opened, which is the book of
life. The dead were judged according to what they had
done as recorded in the books. The sea gave up the dead
that were in it, and death and Hades gave up the dead
that were in them, and each person was judged according
to what they had done. Then death and Hades were
thrown into the lake of fire. The lake of fire is the second
death. Anyone whose name was not found written in the
book of life was thrown into the lake of fire.*

Then I saw "a new heaven and a new earth," for the first heaven and the first earth had passed away, and there was no longer any sea. I saw the Holy City, the new Jerusalem, coming down out of heaven from God, prepared as a bride beautifully dressed for her husband. And I heard a loud voice from the throne saying, "Look! God's dwelling place is now among the people, and he will dwell with them. They will be his people, and God himself will be with them and be their God. He will wipe every tear from their eyes. There will be no more death or mourning or crying or pain, for the old order of things has passed away."

He who was seated on the throne said, "I am making everything new!" Then he said, "Write this down, for these words are trustworthy and true."

He said to me: "It is done. I am the Alpha and the Omega, the Beginning and the End. To the thirsty I will give water without cost from the spring of the water of life. Those who are victorious will inherit all this, and I will be their God and they will be my children. But the cowardly, the unbelieving, the vile, the murderers, the sexually immoral, those who practice magic arts, the idolaters and all liars— they will be consigned to the fiery lake of burning sulfur. This is the second death."

One of the seven angels who had the seven bowls full of the seven last plagues came and said to me, "Come, I will show you the bride, the wife of the Lamb." And he carried me away in the Spirit to a mountain great and high, and showed me the Holy City, Jerusalem, coming down out of heaven from God. It shone with the glory of God, and its brilliance was like that of a very precious jewel, like a jasper, clear as crystal. It had a great, high wall with twelve gates, and with twelve angels at the gates. On the gates were written the names of the twelve tribes of Israel. There were three gates on the east, three on the north, three on the south and three on the west. The wall of the city had twelve foundations, and on them were the names of the twelve apostles of the Lamb.

The angel who talked with me had a measuring rod of gold to measure the city, its gates and its walls. The city was laid out like a square, as long as it was wide. He measured the city with the rod and found it to be 12,000 stadia in length, and as wide and high as it is long. The angel measured the wall using human measurement, and it was 144 cubits thick. The wall was made of jasper, and the city of pure gold, as pure as glass. The foundations of the city walls were decorated with every kind of precious stone. The first foundation was jasper, the second sapphire, the third agate, the fourth emerald, the fifth onyx, the sixth ruby, the seventh chrysolite, the eighth beryl, the ninth topaz, the tenth turquoise, the eleventh jacinth, and the twelfth amethyst. The twelve gates were twelve pearls, each gate made of a single pearl. The great street of the city was of gold, as pure as transparent glass.

I did not see a temple in the city, because the Lord God Almighty and the Lamb are its Temple. The city does not need the sun or the moon to shine on it, for the glory of God gives it light, and the Lamb is its lamp. The nations will walk by its light, and the kings of the earth will bring their splendor into it. On no day will its gates ever be shut, for there will be no night there. The glory and honor of the nations will be brought into it. Nothing impure will ever enter it, nor will anyone who does what is shameful or deceitful, but only those whose names are written in the Lamb's book of life. **Revelation 19-21**

Notes:

_____

_____

_____

_____

_____

_____

_____

_____

_____

_____

_____

_____

_____

_____

12 crops of fruit, which continually produces wholesome and pleasant fruit

*Down the middle of the great street of the city. On each side of the river stood the tree of life, bearing twelve crops of fruit, yielding its fruit every month. And the leaves of the tree are for the healing of the nations. **Revelation 22:2***

In the New Testament, there are also several areas where the number "twelve" appears.

Jesus first spoke in the Temple at 12 years of age

*When he was twelve years old, they went up to the festival, according to the custom. **Luke 2:42***

*"Why were you searching for me?" he asked. "Didn't you know I had to be in my Father's house?" But they did not understand what he was saying to them. Then he went down to Nazareth with them and was obedient to them. But his mother treasured all these things in her heart. And Jesus grew in wisdom and stature, and in favor with God and man. **Luke 2:49-52***

Jesus raised Jarius' 12-year-old daughter from a death-like state

*Immediately the girl stood up and began to walk around (she was twelve years old). At this they were completely astonished. The mention of "twelve" appears in other areas of the New Testament as well. **Mark 5:42***

The multiplication of the loaves and fishes which provided 12 baskets of leftovers.

And he directed the people to sit down on the grass. Taking the five loaves and the two fish and looking up to heaven, he gave thanks and broke the loaves. Then he gave them to the disciples, and the disciples gave them to the people. They all ate and were satisfied, and the disciples picked up twelve basketfuls of broken pieces that were left over. **Matthew 14:19-20**

So they gathered them and filled twelve baskets with the pieces of the five barley loaves left over by those who had eaten. **John 6:13**

The Disciples' faithful obedience would be challenged often. Jesus told the disciples that if they followed him that they would sit on the twelve thrones, judging the twelve tribes of Israel. He also promised them a status reserved for the saints who had suffered persecution on earth for the cause of Christ.

Jesus said to them, "Truly I tell you, at the renewal of all things, when the Son of Man sits on his glorious throne, you who have followed me will also sit on twelve thrones, judging the twelve tribes of Israel." **Matthew 19:28**

The wall of the city had twelve foundations, and on them were the names of the twelve apostles of the Lamb. **Revelation 21:14**

Let us delve into each of the disciples. We want to examine how they were dysfunctional and how their dysfunction relates to our dysfunction. Remember, God calls the dysfunctional. He wants people that can be humble and obedient.

≈ Notes: ≈

_____

_____

_____

_____

_____

_____

_____

_____

_____

_____

_____

_____

_____

_____

_____

_____

The Twelve Disciples
of Christ

Disciple Peter:
(Greek: Petros meaning "Rock")

Peter is the man who was considered the leader of the twelve disciples in the New Testament. Jesus gave Simon the name Peter.

> *These are the twelve he appointed: Simon (to whom he gave the name Peter).* **Mark 3:16**

Simon Peter was born in Bethsaida in AD 1. His dad was Jonah, according to Matthew 16:17, and according to John 1:42, his dad was John. His dad was a fisherman by trade and so was his brother Andrew. Peter was also a fisherman, and it is possible that they partnered in a fishing business with James and John, sons of Zebedee (Luke 5:10). Peter was also married (Mark 1:30). Peter's brother, Andrew, was also a disciple and a follower of John the Baptist (John 1:40) and became a follower of Jesus after hearing the testimony of John the Baptist. Peter owned a house in Capernaum, and this is where Jesus healed his Mother-in-Law.

> *As soon as they left the synagogue, they went with James and John to the home of Simon and Andrew. Simon's*

*mother-in-law was in bed with a fever, and they immediately told Jesus about her. So he went to her, took her hand, and helped her up. The fever left her, and she began to wait on them. **Mark 1:29-31***

*Jesus left the synagogue and went to the home of Simon. Now Simon's mother-in-law was suffering from a high fever, and they asked Jesus to help her. So he bent over her and rebuked the fever, and it left her. She got up at once and began to wait on them. **Luke 4:38-39***

When Jesus saw Peter, he said, "So you are Simon the son of John? You shall be called Cephas, which is translated into Peter," (John 1:42). We do not know how long Peter remained with Jesus at this time. At Jesus's Galilean ministry, he, with the sons of Zebedee, was called by Jesus by the Sea of Galilee, where they were casting their nets into the sea (Matthew 4:18-20). Luke recalls Peter being called in connection with a fishing episode in which, under the instruction of Jesus, Peter and his companions caught a huge number of fish. Peter was still dysfunctional and confessed, "Depart from me, for I am a sinful man, O Lord," (Luke 5:8). From this point on, Peter was a constant companion of Jesus (Matthew 19:27; Mark 10:28; Luke 18:28; John 6:68).

Peter held the position of leadership in the circle of the disciples. He is listed first in the four lists of the twelve disciples in the New Testament (Matthew 10:2; Mark 3:16; Luke 6:14-16; Acts 1:13). Peter is mentioned several times in the Synoptics' common material, for example, the Transfiguration (Matthew 17:1-9; Mark 9:2-10; Luke 9:28-36); in material common to both Matthew and Mark, for example, in the garden of Gethsemane (Matthew 26:37-40; Mark 14:33-38). In Matthew, he attempted walking on water (Matthew 14:28-31). In Mark 11:21, he pointed out the withered fig tree to Jesus. In the book of John, Jesus told Peter to feed my sheep (John 21:15-23). Peter was also one of the three intimate apostles of Jesus. He was often the spokesman for the Twelve (Matthew 15:15; 16:16; Mark 8:29; Luke 9:20; Matthew 18:21; 19:27; Mark 10:28; and Luke 18:28; 12:41). Tax collectors also approached Peter, which was indicative of his leadership role.

> *After Jesus and his disciples arrived in Capernaum, the collectors of the two-drachma temple tax came to Peter and asked, "Doesn't your teacher pay the temple tax?"* **Matthew 17:24**

In the gospel of John, he is referred to the beloved Disciple.

> *So she came running to Simon Peter and the other Disciple, the one Jesus loved, and said, "They have taken the Lord out of the tomb, and we don't know where they have put him!" John 20:2*

There are four times that the inner circle of disciples are alone with Jesus at the Mount of Olives. Here are two examples:

- *As Jesus was sitting on the Mount of Olives opposite the Temple, Peter, James, John and Andrew asked him privately.* **Mark 13:3**
- When Jesus raises a dead girl and heals a sick woman.

Disciple Peter: (Greek: Petros meaning "Rock")

⚜ Notes: ⚜

_____

_____

_____

_____

_____

_____

_____

_____

_____

_____

_____

_____

_____

_____

_____

_____

_____

_____

_____

_____

_____

_____

For Further Examination

He did not let anyone follow him except Peter, James and John the brother of James. **Mark 5:37**

When he arrived at the house of Jairus, he did not let anyone go in with him except Peter, John and James, and the child's father and mother. **Luke 8:51**

Peter also witnessed the Transfiguration of Jesus (Matthew 17:1-9; Mark 9:2-10; Luke 9:28-36). Peter was with Jesus when he was in Gethsemane. Jesus took three disciples, Peter, James, and John with him.

He took Peter and the two sons of Zebedee along with him, and he began to be sorrowful and troubled. **Matthew 26:37**

He took Peter, James and John along with him, and he began to be deeply distressed and troubled. **Mark 14:33**

Jesus scolded Peter for sleeping while he was praying in the garden.

Then he returned to his disciples and found them sleeping. "Couldn't you men keep watch with me for one hour?" he asked Peter. **Matthew 26:40**

Notice that Jesus rebukes Peter by calling him Simon!

Disciple Peter: (Greek: Petros meaning "Rock")

⚜ Notes: ⚜

For Further Examination

Then he returned to his disciples and found them sleeping. "Simon," he said to Peter, "Are you asleep? Couldn't you keep watch for one hour?" **Mark 14:37**

In several places in scripture, you will find that Jesus rebukes Peter by calling him Simon when he is upset with him. In one of the most familiar passages, Peter, when asked by Jesus, "Who am I?" Peter responds as below:

When Jesus came to the region of Caesarea Philippi, he asked his disciples, "Who do people say the Son of Man is?" They replied, "Some say John the Baptist; others say Elijah; and still others, Jeremiah or one of the prophets."

"But what about you?" he asked. "Who do you say I am?"

Simon Peter answered, "You are the Messiah, the Son of the living God."

Jesus replied, "Blessed are you, Simon son of Jonah, for this was not revealed to you by flesh and blood, but by my Father in heaven. And I tell you that you are Peter, and on this rock, I will build my Church, and the gates of Hades will not overcome it. I will give you the keys of the kingdom of heaven; whatever you bind on earth will be bound in heaven, and whatever you loose on earth will be loosed in heaven." Then he ordered his disciples not to tell anyone that he was the Messiah. **Matthew 16:13-20**

I find it interesting that Jesus meant that Peter is the rock upon which Jesus would build His Church. But, yet Peter appears as a man of many contrasts in the gospels. He appears not always to be reliable and stable. For example, following his confession at Caesarea Philippi, he objected violently to Jesus' predictions of his passion. Jesus strongly rebuked him.

❧ Notes: ❧

_____

_____

_____

_____

_____

_____

_____

_____

_____

_____

_____

_____

_____

_____

For Further Examination

Jesus turned and said to Peter, "Get behind me, Satan! You are a stumbling block to me; you do not have in mind the concerns of God, but merely human concerns."
Matthew 16:23

This passage is in striking comparison to the benediction of Jesus in Matthew 16:17.

Jesus replied, "Blessed are you, Simon son of Jonah, for this was not revealed to you by flesh and blood, but by my Father in heaven.
Matthew 16:17

I do not believe, at this time, that Peter understood that Jesus was the Messiah for the world and not just another king replacement. Another demonstration of his dysfunctional behavior is where he attempted to walk on water. He begins with a bold declaration of faith but was frightened as he stepped out of the boat and began to sink. Jesus then rebuked him and asked him why did he doubt? I think that this is a lot like us. We can be very courageous one minute, and the next, the devil gets in our head and we begin to doubt.

"Lord, if it's you," Peter replied, "tell me to come to you on the water." "Come," he said. Then Peter got down out of the boat, walked on the water and came toward Jesus. But when he saw the wind, he was afraid and, beginning to sink, cried out, "Lord, save me!" Immediately Jesus reached out his hand and caught him. "You of little faith," he said, "why did you doubt?" **Matthew 14:28-31**

Disciple Peter: (Greek: Petros meaning "Rock")

❧ Notes: ❧

_____

_____

_____

_____

_____

_____

_____

_____

_____

_____

_____

_____

_____

_____

_____

_____

_____

_____

_____

_____

For Further Examination

There were times when Peter was talking, where he spoke incorrectly. At times he seems to just spew words.

As the men were leaving Jesus, Peter said to him, "Master, it is good for us to be here. Let us put up three shelters— one for you, one for Moses and one for Elijah." (He did not know what he was saying.) **Luke 9:33**

Peter protested during the foot-washing in the Upper Room, and Jesus again had to correct Peter's perspective.

So he got up from the meal, took off his outer clothing, and wrapped a towel around his waist. After that, he poured water into a basin and began to wash his disciples' feet, drying them with the towel that was wrapped around him.

He came to Simon Peter, who said to him, "Lord, are you going to wash my feet?"

Jesus replied, "You do not realize now what I am doing, but later you will understand."

"No," said Peter, "you shall never wash my feet."

Jesus answered, "Unless I wash you, you have no part with me."

"Then, Lord," Simon Peter replied, "not just my feet but my hands and my head as well!"

Jesus answered, "Those who have had a bath need only to

wash their feet; their whole body is clean. And you are clean, though not every one of you." For he knew who was going to betray him, and that was why he said not every one was clean. **John 13:4-11**

Peter was bold and was the first to ask for the identification of the betrayer of Jesus.

⚞ Notes: ⚟

For Further Examination

After he had said this, Jesus was troubled in spirit and testified, "Very truly I tell you, one of you is going to betray me."

His disciples stared at one another, at a loss to know which of them he meant. One of them, the Disciple whom Jesus loved, was reclining next to him. Simon Peter motioned to this Disciple and said, "Ask him which one he means."

Leaning back against Jesus, he asked him, "Lord, who is it?"

Jesus answered, "It is the one to whom I will give this piece of bread when I have dipped it in the dish." Then, dipping the piece of bread, he gave it to Judas, the son of Simon Iscariot. As soon as Judas took the bread, Satan entered into him.

So Jesus told him, "What you are about to do, do quickly." But no one at the meal understood why Jesus said this to him. Since Judas had charge of the money, some thought Jesus was telling him to buy what was needed for the festival, or to give something to the poor. As soon as Judas had taken the bread, he went out. And it was night. **John 13:21-30**

On the way to the Mount of Olives, Peter said that he would be loyal to Jesus. We know that he ended up denying Jesus three times (Matthew 26:30-35; Mark 14:26-31; Luke 22:31-34;

John 13:36-38). During this time, Peter fell asleep while he was to be keeping watch for Jesus while he was praying, cut off the high priest's servant's ear, and denied Jesus three times. For a person that is supposed to be a close follower of Jesus and one of the inner circle, he often spoke without thinking, and Jesus had to set him straight by rebuking him.

Peter was dysfunctional, and he had many issues. Peter would be angry at times, and he was a proud person. He did things without thinking about his actions. So, he was a ready, fire, aim type of person. This is something a lot of us do, and many of us have these traits. Peter, denying his Lord three times, must have caused himself a lot of internal turmoil. He was a proud man, and being told by Jesus that he would deny him three times and then actually doing it was beyond his belief (Matthew 26:69-75; Mark 14:66-72; Luke 22:54-62; John 18:25-27). The three denials were a servant girl saying to him, "You also were with Jesus of Galilee," another servant girl said, "This fellow was with Jesus of Nazareth," and the third time a group of people went up to him and said, "Surely you are one of them; your accent gives you away." Then if this was not bad enough, it announced it to all the disciples when the rooster crows. Can you imagine how he felt during this time? So, in each of these cases, he denied Jesus and then called down curses upon himself.

Then he began to call down curses, and he swore to them, "I don't know the man!" **Matthew 26:74**

The rooster crowing brought Peter to his senses, and his confident boasts meant nothing when faced with danger and harm. He must have been afraid that he, too, maybe taken away. Then to further add insult to injury, Jesus turned and looked at Peter when the rooster crowed.

> *The Lord turned and looked straight at Peter. Then Peter remembered the word the Lord had spoken to him: "Before the rooster crows today, you will disown me three times."*
> **Luke 22:61**

This period must have caused Peter to soul-search and for him to have an introspection. I think he regretted his cowardice that night.

❧ Notes: ☙

_____

_____

_____

_____

_____

_____

_____

_____

_____

_____

For Further Examination

Even with these series of events, Jesus still entrusted Peter with being the leader. The young man at the tomb instructed the women to report to the disciples and Peter.

But go, tell his disciples and Peter, 'He is going ahead of you into Galilee. There you will see him, just as he told you.' **Mark 16:7**

He then appeared to Peter (Cephas) first and then to the group of disciples.

And that he appeared to Cephas, and then to the Twelve. **1 Corinthians 15:5**

The Disciple John reports "the other disciple" and Peter ran to the tomb. Peter displayed his boldness by being the first to go into the tomb. (John 20:2-10) Later, at the Sea of Tiberias when Jesus appeared to the seven disciples, one of them being Peter, Jesus fully restores Peter with the words, "Follow me."

Jesus said this to indicate the kind of death by which Peter would glorify God. Then he said to him, "Follow me!" **John 21:19**

Peter was a vital leader during the early history of the Church as recorded in Acts. Shortly after the ascension of Jesus, Peter led the appointment of a replacement for Judas Iscariot (Acts 1:15-26). He boldly addressed the crowds on Pentecost Sunday and the message he presented was instrumental in the conversion of approximately three thousand people (Acts 2). After Pentecost, Peter performed many different miracles one of them being the healing of a lame man at the Beautiful Gate of the Temple (Acts 3:1-10).

Notes:

For Further Examination

He preached a sermon, which led to his and John's arrest (Acts 4:1-4). The next morning Peter, filled with the Holy Spirit, spoke in court, and they were released with a threat (Acts 4:5-22). This is not the last time that Peter would be the spokesman.

Now a man named Ananias, together with his wife Sapphira, also sold a piece of property. With his wife's full knowledge he kept back part of the money for himself, but brought the rest and put it at the apostles' feet.

Then Peter said, "Ananias, how is it that Satan has so filled your heart that you have lied to the Holy Spirit and have kept for yourself some of the money you received for the land? Didn't it belong to you before it was sold? And after it was sold, wasn't the money at your disposal? What made you think of doing such a thing? You have not lied just to human beings but to God."

When Ananias heard this, he fell down and died. And great fear seized all who heard what had happened. Then some young men came forward, wrapped up his body, and carried him out and buried him.

About three hours later his wife came in, not knowing what had happened. Peter asked her, "Tell me, is this the price you and Ananias got for the land?"

"Yes," she said, "that is the price."

Peter said to her, "How could you conspire to test the Spirit of the Lord? Listen! The feet of the men who buried your husband are at the door, and they will carry you out also."

At that moment she fell down at his feet and died. Then the young men came in and, finding her dead, carried her out and buried her beside her husband. Great fear seized the whole Church and all who heard about these events. Acts 5:1-11

❧ Notes: ❧

_____

_____

_____

_____

_____

_____

_____

_____

_____

_____

_____

_____

_____

For Further Examination

Peter, at the start of his initial work of evangelism, traveled to Samaria. It was here that he rebukes Simon from Samaria.

When the apostles in Jerusalem heard that Samaria had accepted the word of God, they sent Peter and John to Samaria. When they arrived, they prayed for the new believers there that they might receive the Holy Spirit, because the Holy Spirit had not yet come on any of them; they had simply been baptized in the name of the Lord Jesus. Then Peter and John placed their hands on them, and they received the Holy Spirit.

When Simon saw that the Spirit was given at the laying on of the apostles' hands, he offered them money and said, "Give me also this ability so that everyone on whom I lay my hands may receive the Holy Spirit."

Peter answered: "May your money perish with you, because you thought you could buy the gift of God with money! You have no part or share in this ministry, because your heart is not right before God. Repent of this wickedness and pray to the Lord in the hope that he may forgive you for having such a thought in your heart. For I see that you are full of bitterness and captive to sin."

*Then Simon answered, "Pray to the Lord for me so that nothing you have said may happen to me." **Acts 8:14-24***

❧ Notes: ❧

_____

_____

_____

_____

_____

_____

_____

_____

_____

_____

_____

_____

_____

_____

_____

_____

_____

_____

_____

_____

_____

For Further Examination

Later, Peter performed miracles of healing in Lydda and Joppa.

As Peter traveled about the country, he went to visit the Lord's people who lived in Lydda. There he found a man named Aeneas, who was paralyzed and had been bedridden for eight years. "Aeneas," Peter said to him, "Jesus Christ heals you. Get up and roll up your mat." Immediately Aeneas got up. **Acts 9:32-34**

In Joppa there was a disciple named Tabitha (in Greek her name is Dorcas); she was always doing good and helping the poor. About that time she became sick and died, and her body was washed and placed in an upstairs room. Lydda was near Joppa; so when the disciples heard that Peter was in Lydda, they sent two men to him and urged him, "Please come at once!"

Peter went with them, and when he arrived he was taken upstairs to the room. All the widows stood around him, crying and showing him the robes and other clothing that Dorcas had made while she was still with them.

Peter sent them all out of the room; then he got down on his knees and prayed. Turning toward the dead woman, he said, "Tabitha, get up." She opened her eyes, and seeing Peter she sat up. He took her by the hand and helped her to her feet. Then he called for the believers, especially the widows, and presented her to them alive. This became known all over Joppa, and many people believed in the Lord. Peter stayed in Joppa for some time with a tanner named Simon. Acts 9:36-43

Peter, who had grown up in Judaism, still retained the beliefs of Judaism. He struggled between keeping the "Law" and following by faith. It was difficult for him to minister to the Gentiles. Peter still followed the Law of the old testament, as shown in the following passages:

He observed the hour of prayer and attended the Temple regularly (Acts 3:1, Acts 2:46).

He preached and taught in the Temple (Acts 5:42). His ministry was not without controversy from within. In Acts 6:1-6, the internal complaining between the Hellenistic Jews and the Hebraic Jews about their widows being overlooked in the daily distribution of food (Acts 6:1-6). It was the Hellenists that made the Church aware of the implications of the mission mandate of Christ in Acts 1:8.

But you will receive power when the Holy Spirit comes on you; and you will be my witnesses in Jerusalem, and in all Judea and Samaria, and to the ends of the earth. Acts 1:8

It is significant that after the stoning of Steven the Church was dispersed by persecutions, the apostles remained in Jerusalem.

And Saul approved of their killing him. On that day, a great persecution broke out against the Church in Jerusalem, and all except the apostles were scattered throughout Judea and Samaria. Acts 8:1

Peter and John traveled to Samaria as requested by the leaders of the Hellenistic branch of the Church.

*When the apostles in Jerusalem heard that Samaria had accepted the word of God, they sent Peter and John to Samaria. **Acts 8:14***

It was evident that the Pentecost experience did not make Peter fully aware of the Church's perspective. By removing the distinction between clean and unclean, God showed Peter the distinction between Jew and Gentile is gone. This was hard for Peter. Some years later, in Antioch, he limited himself to the Jewish fellowship (Acts 10:1-Acts 10:48). Because of this, Peter received a rebuke from Paul. This happened after the Jerusalem council. (Acts 15). Peter knew better but was still struggling.

When Cephas came to Antioch, I opposed him to his face because he stood condemned. For before certain men came from James, he used to eat with the Gentiles. But when they arrived, he began to draw back and separate himself from the Gentiles because he was afraid of those who belonged to the circumcision group. The other Jews joined him in his hypocrisy so that by their hypocrisy, even Barnabas was led astray.

*When I saw that they were not acting in line with the truth of the gospel, I said to Cephas in front of them all, "You are a Jew, yet you live like a Gentile and not like a Jew. How is it, then, that you force Gentiles to follow Jewish customs?" **Galatians 2:11-14***

❧ Notes: ❧

For Further Examination

After the conversion and baptism of Cornelius at Caesarea, Peter returned to Jerusalem to answer the criticism of the "circumcision party" who had objected to his ministry to the Gentiles.

The apostles and the believers throughout Judea heard that the Gentiles also had received the word of God. So when Peter went up to Jerusalem, the circumcised believers criticized him and said, "You went into the house of uncircumcised men and ate with them."

Starting from the beginning, Peter told them the whole story: "I was in the city of Joppa praying, and in a trance I saw a vision. I saw something like a large sheet being let down from heaven by its four corners, and it came down to where I was. I looked into it and saw four-footed animals of the earth, wild beasts, reptiles and birds. Then I heard a voice telling me, 'Get up, Peter. Kill and eat.'

"I replied, 'Surely not, Lord! Nothing impure or unclean has ever entered my mouth.'

"The voice spoke from heaven a second time, 'Do not call anything impure that God has made clean.' This happened three times, and then it was all pulled up to heaven again.

"Right then three men who had been sent to me from Caesarea stopped at the house where I was staying. The Spirit told me to have no hesitation about going with them. These six brothers also went with me, and we

47

entered the man's house. He told us how he had seen an angel appear in his house and say, 'Send to Joppa for Simon who is called Peter. He will bring you a message through which you and all your household will be saved.'

"As I began to speak, the Holy Spirit came on them as he had come on us at the beginning. Then I remembered what the Lord had said: 'John baptized with water, but you will be baptized with the Holy Spirit.' So if God gave them the same gift he gave us who believed in the Lord Jesus Christ, who was I to think that I could stand in God's way?"

*When they heard this, they had no further objections and praised God, saying, "So then, even to Gentiles God has granted repentance that leads to life." **Acts 11:1-18***

❧ Notes: ❧

_____

_____

_____

_____

_____

_____

_____

_____

_____

For Further Examination

Herod killed James, the brother of John, (John 12:1,2) and imprisoned Peter.

When he saw that this met with approval among the Jews, he proceeded to seize Peter also. This happened during the Festival of Unleavened Bread. 4 After arresting him, he put him in prison, handing him over to be guarded by four squads of four soldiers each. Herod intended to bring him out for public trial after the Passover. So Peter was kept in prison, but the Church was earnestly praying to God for him. Acts 12:3-5

It was after he was imprisoned the angel of the Lord rescued him.

The night before Herod was to bring him to trial, Peter was sleeping between two soldiers, bound with two chains, and sentries stood guard at the entrance. Suddenly an angel of the Lord appeared and a light shone in the cell. He struck Peter on the side and woke him up. "Quick, get up!" he said, and the chains fell off Peter's wrists.

Then the angel said to him, "Put on your clothes and sandals." And Peter did so. "Wrap your cloak around you and follow me," the angel told him. Peter followed him out of the prison, but he had no idea that what the angel was doing was really happening; he thought he was seeing a vision. They passed the first and second guards and came to the iron gate leading to the city. It opened for them by itself, and they went through it. When they had walked the length of one street, suddenly the angel left him.

Then Peter came to himself and said, "Now I know without a doubt that the Lord has sent his angel and rescued me from Herod's clutches and from everything the Jewish people were hoping would happen." **Acts 12:6-11**

✒ Notes: ✒

For Further Examination

After Peter was freed, he went to the house of Mary, where many were in fervent prayer for his deliverance, and he departed and went to another place. The exact place is not referenced.

When this had dawned on him, he went to the house of Mary the mother of John, also called Mark, where many people had gathered and were praying. Peter knocked at the outer entrance, and a servant named Rhoda came to answer the door. When she recognized Peter's voice, she was so overjoyed she ran back without opening it and exclaimed, "Peter is at the door!"

"You're out of your mind," they told her. When she kept insisting that it was so, they said, "It must be his angel."

But Peter kept on knocking, and when they opened the door and saw him, they were astonished. Peter motioned with his hand for them to be quiet and described how the Lord had brought him out of prison. "Tell James and the other brothers and sisters about this," he said, and then he left for another place. Acts 12:12-17

At this point, Peter ceased to be the head of the Jerusalem church, and James "the Just" assumed the leadership (Acts 15:13-21, Acts 21:18). Peter appears once more in Acts at the Jerusalem council (Acts 15) and addressed them.

After much discussion, Peter got up and addressed them: "Brothers, you know that some time ago God made a

choice among you that the Gentiles might hear from my lips the message of the gospel and believe. God, who knows the heart, showed that he accepted them by giving the Holy Spirit to them, just as he did to us. He did not discriminate between us and them, for he purified their hearts by faith. Now then, why do you try to test God by putting on the necks of Gentiles a yoke that neither we nor our ancestors have been able to bear? No! We believe it is through the grace of our Lord Jesus that we are saved, just as they are."
Acts 15:7-11

⚘ Notes: ⚘

_____

_____

_____

_____

_____

_____

_____

_____

_____

_____

_____

For Further Examination

Eusebius dates Peter's death in the fourteenth year of Nero, which would be AD 67-68. This was during the time of the Neuronic persecutions. Jesus spoke about Peter's last days.

Very truly I tell you, when you were younger you dressed yourself and went where you wanted; but when you are old you will stretch out your hands, and someone else will dress you and lead you where you do not want to go.
John 21:18

According to Peter and Eusebius (Bible Gateway; Church History 3:1), Peter insisted on being crucified head-downward. The actual location of the tomb of Peter and his remains have been debated in the 20th century. It is impossible to determine with certainty where his bones are located.

We know that Peter spent the last part of his life in Rome and died a martyr's death. What is more important is that he was dysfunctional and had anger, pride issues, and arrogance. He had to step out of his comfort zone many times, and during these times, he quite often failed and made a fool of himself. He was a human just like us and had the same flaws that we have. Jesus rebuked him several times to keep him in line. He decided to follow Jesus and do whatever he could to spread the good news. Are you willing to step out of your comfort zone and spread the good news no matter what it takes?

❧ Notes: ❧

Disciple John:
(Aramaic/Hebrew – (Yochanan) – Means God Is Gracious)

The Second Disciple that Jesus called was John. His name means grace or mercy of the Lord. John was born in AD 6 in Bethsaida. He is the second most prominent member of the Twelve, was the son of Zebedee, and is one of the best remembered, as witnessed in literature, art, and archeology. There has been more written about John and attributed to him than any of the other twelve disciples. John was a convert of John the Baptist. He met Jesus in the Jordon Valley. (John 1:19-42). At some point after meeting Jesus, he was called by Jesus to follow him, as shown in the gospels (Matthew 4:21; Mark 1:19, 20; Luke 5:10).

In the first three gospels, there is a record that states John had a brother by the name of James, and his father was Zebedee. They were fishermen residing near Capernaum on the Sea of Galilee (Matthew 4:21, 22; Mark 1:19, 20; Luke 5:10). John's mother is believed to be Salome. This is being inferred from a comparison between the two biblical passages (Mark 16:1 and

Matthew 27:56). John and his brother were called the "Sons of Thunder." John was part of the inner circle of Jesus when Jesus raised Jairus' daughter from the dead (Mark 5:37; Luke 8:51). He was at the Transfiguration of Jesus and at the Garden of Gethsemane (Matthew 17:1; Mark 9:2; Luke 9:28; Matthew 26:37; Mark 14:33).

✒ Notes: ✒

_____

_____

_____

_____

_____

_____

_____

_____

_____

_____

_____

_____

_____

_____

For Further Examination

The Bible presents Peter as the leader and the apostles John and James as the other influential ones. Only John is mentioned when asked if they should forbid one who was casting out demons in the name of Jesus.

*"Teacher," said John, "we saw someone driving out demons in your name and we told him to stop, because he was not one of us." **Mark 9:38***

In Acts, John is ranked with Peter as one of the two leaders. John was with Peter at the lame man's healing and was arrested and placed on trial with Peter (Acts 3:1; 4:3-21). John, together with Peter and James, are referred to as pillars in the early Church (Galatians 2:9). Since John is not mentioned by name in the fourth gospel, it is evident that he is the author. John was one of the first two disciples that Jesus recruited (John 1:40). In the last supper with Jesus, he is listed as reclining close to Him. John was the Disciple to ask Jesus who would betray him and learn who the betrayer was.

After he had said this, Jesus was troubled in spirit and testified, "Very truly I tell you, one of you is going to betray me."

His disciples stared at one another, at a loss to know which of them he meant. One of them, the Disciple whom Jesus loved, was reclining next to him. Simon Peter motioned to this Disciple and said, "Ask him which one he means."

Leaning back against Jesus, he asked him, "Lord, who is it?"

Jesus answered, "It is the one to whom I will give this piece of bread when I have dipped it in the dish." Then, dipping the piece of bread, he gave it to Judas, the son of Simon Iscariot. **John 13:21-26**

John was also with Jesus when he was on the cross as he was told to take Jesus' mother home and also at the empty tomb (John 19:26, 27, John 20:2-10). John was the first to recognize Jesus after he rose from the dead.

➤ Notes: ➤

For Further Examination

*Then the Disciple whom Jesus loved said to Peter, "It is the Lord!" As soon as Simon Peter heard him say, "It is the Lord," he wrapped his outer garment around him (for he had taken it off) and jumped into the water. **John 21:7***

Further proof of John writing the book of John is in this passage.

*This is the Disciple who testifies to these things and who wrote them down. We know that his testimony is true. **John 21:24***

It also appears that he wrote the first epistle. The language in the two chapters is similar. Note the common words between the chapters, such as knowledge, world, witness, and life.

*That which was from the beginning, which we have heard, which we have seen with our eyes, which we have looked at and our hands have touched—this we proclaim concerning the Word of life. The life appeared; we have seen it and testify to it, and we proclaim to you the eternal life, which was with the Father and has appeared to us. We proclaim to you what we have seen and heard, so that you also may have fellowship with us. And our fellowship is with the Father and with his Son, Jesus Christ. **1 John 1:1-3***

Notes:

For Further Examination

John suffered from insecurities, just like a lot of us. He was a sophisticated and smart man. He tended to see things in terms of black and white, good and evil. He felt that all people could be put into two categories when it comes to Jesus; a child of God or a child of the devil. He was seeing people either as for Jesus or against. He ruled out those that were unsure. Can you imagine seeing the miracles and not being sure if they were something from the devil? John was able to communicate on any level with anyone, and with intellect, he was able to speak in the simplest of terms when it came to light, darkness, life, water, and bread. John might have been called the brother of James, but he wrote five books of the Bible. That would equate to around 40,000 words. Can you imagine being introduced as James's brother and people continuing to reference you as James's brother even though they knew your name?

John died in AD 100 in an unknown place; most likely it was Ephesus in the Roman Empire. Interestingly, he is the only one of the twelve to die of natural causes.

≈ Notes: ≈

_____

_____

_____

_____

Disciple James:
(Greek: Lakobos Meaning Israel Or He Who Supplants His Brother.)

James (James the Great) was born around AD 3 in Bethsaida, Galilee, in the Roman Empire. James was the son of Zebedee, and his brother was John. He was a fisherman along the Sea of Galilee and in partnership with Peter and Andrew (Mark 4:21; Matthew 17:1; Luke 5:10). They were owners and in charge of many ships and men. The fishermen owned several boats and had hired servants or employees (Mark 1:20; Luke 5:11). John, James's brother, was known to the high priests (John 18:15). It is possible that the family had many hired servants who would allow them to fish in deeper waters and catch a lot more fish than the typical fishermen of the time. When the local markets of Bethsaida and Capernaum had been satisfied, salted fish could have been delivered as far as Jerusalem. Simon and Andrew were most likely partners in the fishing business (Luke 5:10; Mark 1:16). James and John's mother was most likely Salome and some think that this was the sister of Mary, the mother of Jesus (Matthew 27:56; Mark 15:40; John 19:25).

James does not appear to have been with Peter, Andrew, and Zebedee when they went to see John the Baptist. Once the three men returned from Judea, at some point, James became aligned spiritually with the brothers Peter, Andrew, and their dad.

❧ Notes: ☙

_____

_____

_____

_____

_____

_____

_____

_____

_____

_____

_____

_____

_____

_____

_____

_____

For Further Examination

John and James were mending nets when Jesus called them to be disciples. The reason for James the Great was if two people with the same name in a group of friends they would call one "the Great" and one "the Less". James was one of the "Sons of Thunder." John, his brother, was the other. The reason Jesus called them the Boanerges, which means Sons of Thunder (Mark 3:17), was because of how angry they could get. It seems that this was one of their dysfunctions. At one point, they tried to call down heavenly fire on a town (Luke 9:54), but Jesus rebuked them. He also tended to be selfish and prideful. On the last journey to Jerusalem, after he told the twelve disciples what would happen to him, they made the request, "Grant us to sit, one on your right hand and one at your left, in your glory," (Mark 10:37). Their mother also requested the same thing for her sons, talking directly to Jesus (Mark 10:40). Jesus rebuked the request.

Jesus called them together and said, "You know that those who are regarded as rulers of the Gentiles lord it over them, and their high officials exercise authority over them. Not so with you. Instead, whoever wants to become great among you must be your servant, and whoever wants to be first must be slave of all. For even the Son of Man did not come to be served, but to serve, and to give his life as a ransom for many." Mark 10:42-45

There are not too many accounts of James in the Bible. Most of the time, John did not mention his brother by name, but he would reveal his identity in other ways. James occupied a high place within the disciples. He stands second or third in the names mentioned and always was in company of Andrew, John, and Peter. He was also one of the confidants of Jesus (Matthew 10:2; Mark 3:17; Luke 6:14; Acts 1:13). James was at the house of Jairus when his child was raised from the dead (Mark 5:37; Luke 8:51). At the Transfiguration, when they climbed the mountain with Jesus (Matthew 17:1; Mark 9:2: Luke 9:28).

❧ Notes: ☙

_____

_____

_____

_____

_____

_____

_____

_____

_____

_____

_____

_____

For Further Examination

James's presence was mentioned on these two other occasions in the Bible. One was at the Mount of Olives.

As Jesus was sitting on the Mount of Olives opposite the Temple, Peter, James, John and Andrew asked him privately, "Tell us, when will these things happen? And what will be the sign that they are all about to be fulfilled?"
Mark 13:3-4

He was also present at the Sea of Galilee when the risen Lord appeared to the disciples for the third time.

Afterward Jesus appeared again to his disciples, by the Sea of Galilee. It happened this way: Simon Peter, Thomas (also known as Didymus), Nathanael from Cana in Galilee, the sons of Zebedee, and two other disciples were together. "I'm going out to fish," Simon Peter told them, and they said, "We'll go with you." So they went out and got into the boat, but that night they caught nothing.

Early in the morning, Jesus stood on the shore, but the disciples did not realize that it was Jesus.

He called out to them, "Friends, haven't you any fish?"

"No," they answered.

He said, "Throw your net on the right side of the boat and you will find some." When they did, they were unable to haul the net in because of the large number of fish.

Then the Disciple whom Jesus loved said to Peter, "It is the Lord!" As soon as Simon Peter heard him say, "It is the Lord," he wrapped his outer garment around him (for he had taken it off) and jumped into the water. The other disciples followed in the boat, towing the net full of fish, for they were not far from shore, about a hundred yards. When they landed, they saw a fire of burning coals there with fish on it, and some bread.

Jesus said to them, "Bring some of the fish you have just caught." So Simon Peter climbed back into the boat and dragged the net ashore. It was full of large fish, 153, but even with so many the net was not torn. Jesus said to them, "Come and have breakfast." None of the disciples dared ask him, "Who are you?" They knew it was the Lord. Jesus came, took the bread and gave it to them, and did the same with the fish. This was now the third time Jesus appeared to his disciples after he was raised from the dead.
John 21:1-14

❧ Notes: ❧

_____

_____

_____

_____

_____

For Further Examination

We assume that James was also present many other times where his name is not explicitly mentioned.

I have always said I would like to control the lightning bolts, but I know God won't allow this as I would be tempted to use them unwisely. I could think of a few people that are deserving of one right now! I am not judging those people, but I think they could use a little positive encouragement, that's all. Ok, I admit I still need some work in this area also. It seems that back then James also had some of the same issues I wrestle with today.

James was called the first martyr among the apostles. King Herod Agrippa made James the first target in his attack upon the Church, which also included Peter's arrest. James was put to death with a sword in Jerusalem. James died about AD 62 for his faith.

It was about this time that King Herod arrested some who belonged to the Church, intending to persecute them. He had James, the brother of John, put to death with the sword. When he saw that this met with approval among the Jews, he proceeded to seize Peter also. This happened during the Festival of Unleavened Bread. Acts 12:1-3

It is possible, since James appeared to be singled out, that he was part of a select group among the Church leaders at Jerusalem, similar to the followers of Jesus. If James was among the prominent, he was also most likely among the most feared and hated Christians. James's death fulfilled the prophecy of Jesus that he too should drink of his Master's cup.

"We can," they answered.

*Jesus said to them, "You will drink the cup I drink and be baptized with the baptism I am baptized with." **Mark 10:39***

❧ Notes: ☙

_____

_____

_____

_____

_____

_____

_____

_____

_____

_____

_____

_____

_____

_____

_____

_____

_____

Disciple Andrew:
(Greek: Andrew – Meaning Manly.)

Andrew was the brother of Simon Peter and one of the first disciples to be called by Jesus. He was born in Galilee in the Roman Empire sometime around AD 5 to AD 10. He was the son of Jonah (John) (Matthew 16:17). He lived in Bethsaida in Galilee (John 1:44; John 12:21). Andrew is a native of Galilee who spoke Greek as well as Aramaic. He was strongly influenced by the Gentile culture (to us, this would be the secular culture of today). Andrew shared the home of Simon, his brother, and they lived in Capernaum (Mark 1:21; Mark 1:29). He was employed as a fisherman on the Sea of Galilee (Matthew 4:18). Simon and Andrew worked in a partnership with James and John, the sons of Zebedee (Luke 5:10). Andrew set aside his work to see John the Baptist when he was preaching at Bethany (John 1:28). John the Baptist reached Andrew, and he began following him. It was here that he committed himself to Jesus (John 1:35, 40). When James heard John the Baptist preach, he wanted to reach out to Jesus and talk to him. The interview with Jesus that day convinced Andrew that Jesus was the expected Messiah.

The next day John was there again with two of his disciples. When he saw Jesus passing by, he said, "Look, the Lamb of God!"

When the two disciples heard him say this, they followed Jesus. Turning around, Jesus saw them following and asked, "What do you want?"

They said, "Rabbi" (which means "Teacher"), "where are you staying?"

"Come," he replied, "and you will see." So they went and saw where he was staying, and they spent that day with him. It was about four in the afternoon. **John 1:35-39**

✺ Notes: ✺

_____

_____

_____

_____

_____

_____

_____

_____

_____

_____

_____

For Further Examination

Andrew was very enthusiastic and searched for his brother, Simon, to share the message of Jesus with him. He talked to Peter and brought him into contact with Jesus, and this was the turning point in Peter's life.

> *Andrew, Simon Peter's brother, was one of the two who heard what John had said and who had followed Jesus. The first thing Andrew did was to find his brother Simon and tell him, "We have found the Messiah" (that is, the Christ). And he brought him to Jesus.*
>
> *Jesus looked at him and said, "You are Simon son of John. You will be called Cephas" (which, when translated, is Peter).* **John 1:40-42**

It is likely that other followers, along with Andrew, were at Bethany and remained with Jesus during the events in the following passage (John 1:43-4:54). Andrew participated in these events and also assisted in the baptizing of the people that is recorded in John (John 3:22; John 4:2).

When Jesus returned to Galilee, Andrew went back to work as a fisherman. Once Jesus had established his ministry in Capernaum, he called Andrew, Peter, James, and John to be "fishers of men" (Matthew 4:13; Matthew 4:18-22; Mark 1:16-20; Luke 5:1-11).

At a later time, Andrew was among the Twelve that Jesus selected to be his apostles (Mark 3:18; Luke 6:14). In these lists (Matthew 10:2-4; Mark 3:16-19; Luke 6:14-16; Acts 1:13),

Andrew was named among the disciples' first four. In the private inquiry of Jesus' predictions for the future, he was listed with Peter, James, and John (Mark 13:3, Mark 13:4). It appears that Andrew was just on the fringe of the inner circle of the disciples.

✦ Notes: ✦

For Further Examination

Before the feeding of the five thousand, Peter stood in contrast to Philip. Philip wanted to know basically how could they afford to feed this large group of people, where Andrew pointed out the boy with five small barley loaves and two small fish.

The Jewish Passover Festival was near.

When Jesus looked up and saw a great crowd coming toward him, he said to Philip, "Where shall we buy bread for these people to eat?" He asked this only to test him, for he already had in mind what he was going to do.

Philip answered him, "It would take more than half a year's wages to buy enough bread for each one to have a bite!"

Another of his disciples, Andrew, Simon Peter's brother, spoke up, "Here is a boy with five small barley loaves and two small fish, but how far will they go among so many?"
John 6:4-9

❧ Notes: ❧

For Further Examination

At the last Passover, Philip went to Andrew at the request of some Greeks for an interview with Jesus. Andrew concluded that Jesus should decide whether or not to grant the interview.

Now there were some Greeks among those who went up to worship at the festival. They came to Philip, who was from Bethsaida in Galilee, with a request. "Sir," they said, "we would like to see Jesus." Philip went to tell Andrew; Andrew and Philip in turn told Jesus. **John 12:20-22**

Andrew is mentioned among those who waited in the Upper Room after Jesus's ascension. After this, Andrew's name completely disappears from the New Testament.

When they arrived, they went upstairs to the room where they were staying. Those present were Peter, John, James and Andrew; Philip and Thomas, Bartholomew and Matthew; James son of Alphaeus and Simon the Zealot, and Judas son of James. **Acts 1:13**

Notes:

For Further Examination

Andrew did not possess the ability to lead like his brother Peter. He was content to blend in and play a role behind the scenes. He had common sense and could determine what the next step should be. We would consider him to be an introvert. He seems to be more neutral and could take or leave it. He was happy behind the scenes. Andrew was not bound by traditional views and was open to a new truth. Being a man of convictions, he was eager to have others share what he had come to know. He spent his time bringing others in touch with his Master. He has been called "not only the first home missionary but also the first foreign Missionary" (John 1:41; John 12:22) (G. Milligan, HDCG, I, 53).

Jesus can use all of us who are willing to be the hands and feet of Jesus. It does not matter what we think as much as it does what Jesus knows. Even though Andrew was a quiet man, he still served God's purpose.

It is believed that Andrew was martyred at Patras being bound to an X-shaped cross in AD 60.

～ Notes: ～

_____

_____

_____

_____

Disciple Philip:
(Greek – Philippos, Meaning 'Lover Of Horses')

Philip was born in Bethsaida Galilee in AD 3. He was a close friend of Andrew and Peter and also a native of Bethsaida. Jesus called Philip where John the Baptist was preaching near Bethany. Philip is the one that brought Nathaniel to Jesus (John 1:44, John 1:43; John 1:45-51). He was most likely first a disciple of John the Baptist.

> *The next day Jesus decided to leave for Galilee. Finding Philip, he said to him, "Follow me." John 1:43*

Was Philip the one that asked permission to go and bury his father before leaving with Jesus to be a disciple?

> *Another disciple said to him, "Lord, first let me go and bury my father." Matthew 8:21*

> *He said to another man, "Follow me."*

> *But he replied, "Lord, first let me go and bury my father." Luke 9:59*

Notes:

For Further Examination

It is interesting here that Jesus did wait for him. He is also portrayed as an introvert. He was shy, maybe naïve, and timid. He was courageous enough to let Nathanael know that he had discovered the Messiah as foretold in the Old Testament.

*Philip found Nathanael and told him, "We have found the one Moses wrote about in the Law, and about whom the prophets also wrote—Jesus of Nazareth, the son of Joseph." **John 1:45***

Jesus tested Philip at the miracle of the loaves and fishes by asking him how we could purchase bread so that the people could eat (John 6:5). Maybe it was his responsibility to provide food, or his faith may have been weak.

Philip could have received his name in Greek from Philip the Tetrarch (Luke 3:1). This could also explain why the Greeks at Passover sought him out on Palm Sunday.

Now there were some Greeks among those who went up to worship at the festival. 21 They came to Philip, who was from Bethsaida in Galilee, with a request. "Sir," they said, "we would like to see Jesus." Philip went to tell Andrew; Andrew and Philip in turn told Jesus.

*Jesus replied, "The hour has come for the Son of Man to be glorified." **John 12:20-23***

✖ Notes: ✖

For Further Examination

Philip failed to wholeheartedly believe in the kingdom because he failed to understand it. We have similar issues as it is hard to understand at times, but he had an advantage that we do not, Jesus was there. He did not understand about Heaven (John 14:1-9). Despite these failures, he acquired a missionary spirit and was instrumental in leading others to Christ. First, he was anxious about 200 denarii to buy bread in the presence of the Bread of Life. Second, he sought additional revelation ("Show us the Father," John 14:8) when the substance of the incarnation already had been given him. Yet amid insufficient knowledge and imperfect spiritual insight, he acquired a true missionary spirit. He was mentioned as being in the group that was in the Upper Room and were awaiting the coming of the Holy Spirit.

> *When they arrived, they went upstairs to the room where they were staying. Those present were Peter, John, James and Andrew; Philip and Thomas, Bartholomew and Matthew; James son of Alphaeus and Simon the Zealot, and Judas son of James. Acts 1:13*

Philip is believed to have spent the latter part of his life in Phrygia and died at Hierapolis by hanging in AD 80.

Notes:

Disciple Bartholomew:
(Greek – Bartholomaios Meaning Son Of Talmai).

Bartholomew was born in the 1 century AD in Cana, Galilee, the Roman Empire. He is in all the four lists of the disciples in the New Testament (Matthew 10:3; Mark 3:18; Luke 6:14; Acts 1:13). There is not a whole lot that is known about him. It is possible that he was a fisherman who joined the first five disciples. After Jesus was crucified it is possible that he returned to fishing.

> *Simon Peter, Thomas (also known as Didymus), Nathanael (Bartholomew) from Cana in Galilee, the sons of Zebedee, and two other disciples were together. "I'm going out to fish," Simon Peter told them, and they said, "We'll go with you." So they went out and got into the boat, but that night they caught nothing.* **John 21:2-3**

Bartholomew left behind everything to follow Jesus. He is believed to be a missionary to India, Phrygia, and Armenia. He died in the 1st century AD, possibly at Albanopolis, after perhaps being skinned alive.

⚬ Notes: ⚬

Disciple Thomas (Didymus):
(Greek –Thomas From Aramaic – Te'oma Meaning 'Twin')

Thomas was born in the 1st century AD in Galilee, the Roman Province of Judea. Thomas is one of the 12 disciples (Matthew 10:3; Mark 3:18; Luke 6:15; Acts 1:13). Thomas is primarily in the gospel of John. He, at times, is wishy-washy. For example, when Jesus wanted to go to Judea to heal Lazarus, Thomas was both wanting to be loyal but was also pessimistic when he said, "Let us also go, that we may die with him." The disciples feared that they would be stoned (John 11:16). Jesus assumed that the disciples knew the way to the Father's house—that being the way to heaven. Thomas being honest and forthright, confessed that they did not know where Jesus was going; so how could they know the way (John 14:5). On the evening of the resurrection, Thomas was not with the other disciples when Jesus first appeared. When the disciples told Thomas that they had seen Jesus, he doubted and told them unless he could see and touch Jesus, he would not believe.

So the other disciples told him, "We have seen the Lord!"

But he said to them, "Unless I see the nail marks in his hands and put my finger where the nails were, and put my hand into his side, I will not believe."

Thomas, at this point, was called doubting Thomas. When Jesus appeared again eight days later, he believed and uttered, "My Lord and my God!" **John 20:25**

Thomas said to him, "My Lord and my God!" **John 20:28**

⚜ Notes: ⚜

_____

_____

_____

_____

_____

_____

_____

_____

_____

For Further Examination

Thomas was fishing on the Sea of Galilee with six other disciples, and they had caught nothing. Jesus appeared to them the third time after his resurrection.

Afterward Jesus appeared again to his disciples, by the Sea of Galilee. It happened this way: Simon Peter, Thomas (also known as Didymus, Nathanael from Cana in Galilee, the sons of Zebedee, and two other disciples were together. "I'm going out to fish," Simon Peter told them, and they said, "We'll go with you." So they went out and got into the boat, but that night they caught nothing. Early in the morning, Jesus stood on the shore, but the disciples did not realize that it was Jesus.

He called out to them, "Friends, haven't you any fish?"

"No," they answered.

He said, "Throw your net on the right side of the boat and you will find some." When they did, they were unable to haul the net in because of the large number of fish.

Then the Disciple whom Jesus loved said to Peter, "It is the Lord!" As soon as Simon Peter heard him say, "It is the Lord," he wrapped his outer garment around him (for he had taken it off) and jumped into the water. The other disciples followed in the boat, towing the net full of fish, for they were not far from shore, about a hundred yards. When they landed, they saw a fire of burning coals there with fish on it, and some bread.

Jesus said to them, "Bring some of the fish you have just caught." So Simon Peter climbed back into the boat and dragged the net ashore. It was full of large fish, 153, but even with so many the net was not torn. Jesus said to them, "Come and have breakfast." None of the disciples dared ask him, "Who are you?" They knew it was the Lord. Jesus came, took the bread and gave it to them, and did the same with the fish. This was now the third time Jesus appeared to his disciples after he was raised from the dead.
John 21:1-14

✢ Notes: ✢

_____

_____

_____

_____

_____

_____

_____

_____

For Further Examination

The last time that Thomas was mentioned in the New Testament was after Jesus's ascension. The 11 were gathered in a prayer meeting with some women, Mary the mother of Jesus and His brethren.

> *Then the apostles returned to Jerusalem from the hill called the Mount of Olives, a Sabbath day's walk from the city. When they arrived, they went upstairs to the room where they were staying. Those present were Peter, John, James and Andrew; Philip and Thomas, Bartholomew and Matthew; James son of Alphaeus and Simon the Zealot, and Judas son of James. They all joined together constantly in prayer, along with the women and Mary the mother of Jesus, and with his brothers. **Acts 1:12-14***

Some believe Thomas was martyred, run through with a lance, while others think that he died of natural causes. He is believed to have been killed in AD 72. Thomas is remembered as "Doubting Thomas." His faith, like ours, comes into question at times. We all have periods of time that we struggle with certain things. Faith is one of the biggest struggles we have. Believing in what we cannot see is very hard at times.

❧ Notes: ❧

Disciple Matthew (Levi):
(Greek – Maththaios –
Meaning 'Gift Of Yahweh')

Matthew was born in the first century AD in Capernaum. He was a Jewish tax collector, also called a revenue officer of Capernaum. Tax collectors (publicans) were despised and regarded as traitors to their people. The money was considered unclean, and those paying the tax would avoid asking for change. The money of a tax collector could not be tithed to the Temple, and they were forbidden to testify in court. A good Jew would not associate with a publican in private life. When Jesus ate at Matthew's house, this upset the Pharisees (Matthew 9:10-13). Matthew was also called Levi and was called to be a disciple by Jesus while sitting at the tax office (Matthew 9:9; 10:3; Mark 2:14; Acts 1:13). We often hear "The Gospel According to Matthew" because the name Matthew first appears in the New Testament.

> *As Jesus went on from there, he saw a man named Matthew sitting at the tax collector's booth. "Follow me,"* *he told him, and Matthew got up and followed him.*
> ***Matthew 9:9***

As an apostle in Matthew's gospel, he is listed as "Matthew the tax collector" and is listed as the 8th disciple after Peter, Andrew, James, John, Philip, Bartholomew, and Thomas.

> *Jesus called his twelve disciples to him and gave them authority to drive out impure spirits and to heal every disease and sickness. These are the names of the twelve apostles: first, Simon (who is called Peter) and his brother Andrew; James son of Zebedee, and his brother John; Philip and Bartholomew; Thomas and Matthew the tax collector; James son of Alphaeus, and Thaddaeus; Simon the Zealot and Judas Iscariot, who betrayed him.* **Matthew 10:1-4**

❧ Notes: ❧

_____

_____

_____

_____

_____

_____

_____

_____

_____

For Further Examination

In the other lists of the twelve disciples, Levi is listed as "Matthew." Both Mark and Luke also identify him as "Levi." Matthew is believed to have written the first gospel. In the Gospel of Matthew, he boldly calls himself "Matthew the tax collector" (Matthew 10:3). Since Matthew was a tax collector, he was accustomed to keeping excellent records, and this would have aided him in writing the detailed gospel of Matthew. Since all three of the synoptic gospels record the calling of Matthew (Levi), we can conclude his calling to be a disciple of Jesus was a great event in his life. It is also remarkable because most tax collectors (publicans) were considered to be of the lowest state among the Jews. They were classified in the same category as thieves and harlots.

Tax collectors are servants of Rome's hated government and were under such men as Herod the Great. They were known for high taxes, extortion, and other stern methods of ruling the people. Often, revenue men would purchase the tax franchise for a district and collect revenue of all sorts, earning a high commission. Because Matthew was a Jew, this made matters worse as he was considered to be a turncoat and renegade by his own people. Jesus calling him one of the twelve disciples' shows that he was an outstanding symbol of the Christian Church where people were called to follow, repent, and have faith.

In Jesus's parable of the two sons, Jesus preaches that the people did not believe him, but the tax collectors and harlots believed him. Even when they saw miracles, the people did not repent and believe.

"What do you think? There was a man who had two sons. He went to the first and said, 'Son, go and work today in the vineyard.' 'I will not,' he answered, but later he changed his mind and went.

"Then the father went to the other son and said the same thing. He answered, 'I will, sir,' but he did not go.

"Which of the two did what his father wanted?"

'The first,' they answered."

Jesus said to them, "Truly I tell you, the tax collectors and the prostitutes are entering the kingdom of God ahead of you. For John came to you to show you the way of righteousness, and you did not believe him, but the tax collectors and the prostitutes did. And even after you saw this, you did not repent and believe him." **Matthew 21:28-32**

⚓ Notes: ⚓

_____

_____

_____

_____

_____

_____

For Further Examination

The first three gospels record that immediately after his calling, Matthew held a dinner for his tax collector friends and Jesus, along with the disciples. This was a high point at the beginning of the missionary thrust of the Church. Levi (Matthew) knew what it was like to be an outcast of society. Even though he had attempted to turn back to the normal society of the time, the way was blocked. He knew what it was like to be separated from his people and become a member of the underworld in which they lived and operated.

> *While Jesus was having dinner at Matthew's house, many tax collectors and sinners came and ate with him and his disciples. When the Pharisees saw this, they asked his disciples, "Why does your teacher eat with tax collectors and sinners?"*
>
> *On hearing this, Jesus said, "It is not the healthy who need a doctor, but the sick. But go and learn what this means: 'I desire mercy, not sacrifice.' For I have not come to call the righteous, but sinners."* **Matthew 9:10-14**

Jesus is talking about the people that need a physician. Those people are sick, and Jesus is coming to call the "sick," not the righteous. The interesting thing is that Luke records the house as Matthew's and not Jesus's house where the dinner was held. Matthew had deep convictions, and he wanted others to come to Jesus. Jesus calling a tax collector to be a disciple had to have his followers amazed as well as the Pharisees. The Pharisees did not like tax collectors, which would have added to hostile actions against Jesus and the disciples. The Gospel of Matthew contains some of the most scathing rebukes of the Pharisees (Matthew 23:1-37). In these verses, he harshly rebukes the teachers of the law and the Pharisees, calling them hypocrites, blind guides. He condemns them for being self-righteous. He calls them snakes and the brood of vipers.

> *Then Jesus said to the crowds and to his disciples: "The teachers of the law and the Pharisees sit in Moses" seat. So you must be careful to do everything they tell you. But do not do what they do, for they do not practice what they preach. They tie up heavy, cumbersome loads and put them on other people's shoulders, but they themselves are not willing to lift a finger to move them.*

> *"Everything they do is done for people to see: They make their phylacteries wide and the tassels on their garments long; they love the place of honor at banquets and the most important seats in the synagogues; they love to be greeted with respect in the marketplaces and to be called 'Rabbi'' by others.*

> *"But you are not to be called 'Rabbi, for you have one Teacher, and you are all brothers. And do not call anyone on earth 'father,' for you have one Father, and he is in heaven. Nor are you to be called instructors, for you have one Instructor, the Messiah. The greatest among you will be your servant. For those who exalt themselves will be humbled, and those who humble themselves will be exalted.*

"Woe to you, teachers of the law and Pharisees, you hypocrites! You shut the door of the kingdom of heaven in people's faces. You yourselves do not enter, nor will you let those enter who are trying to.

"Woe to you, teachers of the law and Pharisees, you hypocrites! You travel over land and sea to win a single convert, and when you have succeeded, you make them twice as much a child of hell as you are.

"Woe to you, blind guides! You say, 'If anyone swears by the temple, it means nothing; but anyone who swears by the gold of the temple is bound by that oath.' You blind fools! Which is greater: the gold, or the Temple that makes the gold sacred? You also say, 'If anyone swears by the altar, it means nothing; but anyone who swears by the gift on the altar is bound by that oath.' You blind men! Which is greater: the gift, or the altar that makes the gift sacred? Therefore, anyone who swears by the altar swears by it and by everything on it. And anyone who swears by the Temple swears by it and by the one who dwells in it. And anyone who swears by heaven swears by God's throne and by the one who sits on it.

"Woe to you, teachers of the law and Pharisees, you hypocrites! You give a tenth of your spices—mint, dill and cumin. But you have neglected the more important matters of the law—justice, mercy and faithfulness. You should have practiced the latter, without neglecting the former. You blind guides! You strain out a gnat but swallow a camel.

"Woe to you, teachers of the law and Pharisees, you hypocrites! You clean the outside of the cup and dish, but inside they are full of greed and self-indulgence. Blind Pharisee! First clean the inside of the cup and dish, and then the outside also will be clean.

"Woe to you, teachers of the law and Pharisees, you hypocrites! You are like whitewashed tombs, which look beautiful on the outside but on the inside are full of the bones of the dead and everything unclean. In the same way, on the outside you appear to people as righteous but on the inside you are full of hypocrisy and wickedness.

"Woe to you, teachers of the law and Pharisees, you hypocrites! You build tombs for the prophets and decorate the graves of the righteous. And you say, 'If we had lived in the days of our ancestors, we would not have taken part with them in shedding the blood of the prophets.' So you testify against yourselves that you are the descendants of those who murdered the prophets. Go ahead, then, and complete what your ancestors started!

"You snakes! You brood of vipers! How will you escape being condemned to hell? Therefore I am sending you prophets and sages and teachers. Some of them you will kill and crucify; others you will flog in your synagogues and pursue from town to town. And so upon you will come all the righteous blood that has been shed on earth, from the blood of righteous Abel to the blood of Zechariah son of Berekiah, whom you murdered between the Temple and the altar. Truly I tell you, all this will come on this generation.

*"Jerusalem, Jerusalem, you who kill the prophets and stone those sent to you, how often I have longed to gather your children together, as a hen gathers her chicks under her wings, and you were not willing." **Matthew 23:1-37***

Matthew is known most of all within the Church for writing the first gospel. This gospel reaches all the people from the Gentile to the Jew, the righteous to the unrighteous. This gospel has something for everyone. Matthew died by sword in the 1st Century AD near Hierapolis or Ethiopia.

⚜ Notes: ⚜

_____

_____

_____

_____

_____

_____

_____

_____

_____

_____

_____

_____

_____

Disciple James:
James The Less

James (James the Less) was born in the 1st century BC. He was the son of Alphaeus (Matthew 9:9; Mark 2:14). He is only mentioned a few places in the Bible and not much is known about him (Matthew 10:3; Mark 3:18; Luke 6:15; Acts 1:13). Many people believe that he is the same person as James the Younger and most likely was a tradesman of some sort. He headed the third group of four disciples in each of the lists of the Twelve, being together with Thaddaeus in Matthew and Mark and with Simon the Zealot in Luke and Acts. Many people believe that he was also called James the younger. If this is true then he would be known as the son of Mary and the brother of Joseph. His mother, Mary, is mentioned as being present at the crucifixion and discovering the empty tomb (Matthew 27:56; Mark 15:40; Mark 16:1; Luke 24:10).

Legend has it that he was stoned by the Jews for preaching Christ and was buried next to the sanctuary in Jerusalem. He died in 62 AD (Budge, Contending's of the Apostles, II, 50, 264-266).

� Notes: ✑

Disciple Thaddaeus:
(Jude)

Thaddaeus was born in the 1st century AD in Galilee. He was a tradesman of some sort. He is mentioned in two of the four lists of Jesus' disciples (Matthew 10:3, Mark 3:18). He was also referred to as Jude of James, Jude Thaddaeus, Judas Thaddaeus, or Lebbaeus. Nothing else is known about him other than the mention in the two lists of the disciples. He died in the 1st century AD in Armenia, possibly being killed by bow and arrow.

❧ Notes: ❧

_____

_____

_____

_____

_____

Disciple Simon The Zealot:
(Greek: God Has Heard).

Simon was born in the 1st century AD in Cana Galilee. Simon was also called "the Cananaean". He was a Zealot (gang member). He was fiercely loyal to his faith and Israel. Zealots were a religious sect (zelotes) and were a gang that would arouse rebellion among the Jews. They would carry knives and attack those they were rebelling against. He insisted that the Jews must rebel against the Romans. Simon engaged in politics and anarchy in hopes of instigating a revolution that would overthrow the Roman government. He joined Jesus as a disciple, even though he remained zealous, but with his loyalty and allegiance to Jesus instead of political revolution. Having zealot as part of your name meant that you were not liked very much, and he would express his worldly views every chance he could (Matthew 10:4, Mark 3:18). Simon died in the 1st or 2nd century. The place of his death is still disputed but it is believed he was crucified in modern-day Iran.

⚬ Notes: ⚬

Disciple Judas Iscariot:
'Iscariot' Is From The Hebrew Word 'Ish Kerioth' Meaning 'A Man From Kerioth'

There is nothing known about Judas Iscariot's early life. He is first mentioned in the choosing of the twelve, at which point all the Synoptics add the clause, "who betrayed him" (Matthew 10:4; Mark 3:19; Luke 6:16). His relation to Jesus is not mentioned until Bethany when Mary anointed Jesus with the expensive ointment (perfume). Judas protested that this gift was a waste; had the ointment been sold, the proceeds would have become available to him as he was the treasurer of the Twelve (Matthew 26:6-13; Mark 14:3-10; John 12:1-8).

It is believed that this rebuking caused Judas to go to the chief priests to bargain for the betrayal (Luke 22:3). In John's book, it states that Judas withdrew from the meal in the Upper Room to complete the deal (John 13:26-30). The motivation for the betrayal is not stated in the gospels. He most likely believed that Jesus was the promised Messiah, and Jesus would rescue Israel from the Gentiles (Matthew 19:27; 20:20-23; Luke 24:21; Acts 1:6). Judas planned the capture out. Not only did he arrange the capture, but he also identified him in the garden of Gethsemane, where Jesus was arrested (Matthew 26:47; Mark 14:43; Luke 22:47; John 18:3-5). When Jesus was condemned to death, Judas, being overwhelmed with remorse, attempted to undo the evil deed and return the money.

When Judas, who had betrayed him, saw that Jesus was condemned, he was seized with remorse and returned the thirty pieces of silver to the chief priests and the elders. "I have sinned," he said, "for I have betrayed innocent blood."

"What is that to us?" they replied. "That's your responsibility."

So Judas threw the money into the Temple and left. Then he went away and hanged himself. **Matthew 27:3-5**

With the payment he received for his wickedness, Judas bought a field; there he fell headlong, his body burst open and all his intestines spilled out. **Acts 1:18**

Notes:

_____

_____

_____

_____

_____

For Further Examination

Later, the priests used the money to buy the potter's field and it was called "The Field of Blood" as a place to bury strangers.

*The chief priests picked up the coins and said, "It is against the law to put this into the treasury, since it is blood money." So they decided to use the money to buy the potter's field as a burial place for foreigners. That is why it has been called the Field of Blood to this day. **Matthew 27:6-8***

So this is confusing. It is believed the priests bought the property on behalf of Judas. It was Judas's money and the priests used it to buy the field, because they could not use the blood money in the temple treasury. Thus Judas did purchase the field.

Judas betrayed Jesus for a small sum of money. Who of us would do something similar if we were to face death or torture?

❧ Notes: ❧

Disciple Matthias:
(Greek: Gift Of Yahweh)

Matthias was born in the 1st century AD in Judaea, part of the Roman Empire. He was chosen to take the place of Judas Iscariot.

> *So they nominated two men: Joseph called Barsabbas (also known as Justus) and Matthias. Then they prayed, "Lord, you know everyone's heart. Show us which of these two you have chosen to take over this apostolic ministry, which Judas left to go where he belongs." Then they cast lots, and the lot fell to Matthias; so he was added to the eleven apostles. Acts 1:23-26*

The process of selecting this Disciple was different from all the others. The two men were recommended by the "hundred and twenty," not by the 11 apostles (Acts 1:15). These men had to have the necessary qualifications for apostleship. These men had to be followers of Jesus, baptized, and had to have encountered the risen Lord. To make sure they had a divine selection, they prayed, and then the sacred lot was cast as had been done in the Old Testament. We are not sure about his death. Some believe that he was either martyred in Judea or that he evangelized the Ethiopians. He died in AD 80.

❧ Notes: ❧

Conclusion:

These disciples and their dysfunctions give people hope for today. All the disciples were in some way dysfunctional.

Peter denied Jesus three times.

Thomas did not believe and doubted that he had arisen.

Jesus's main disciples fell asleep when Jesus most needed them.

Judas betrayed him and gave him up to the government for a small amount of money.

Jesus told the disciples to wait in Jerusalem after his death; instead, they went their own ways and returned to their previous occupations.

When Jesus needed the disciples the most is when they were the most dysfunctional.

In John 6, a lot of the disciples left him after a very demanding sermon on discipleship. Only the twelve remained.

Conclusion:

❧ Notes: ❧

For Further Examination

Just think and picture Jesus dying on the cross, and when he looks down at his feet, there are few people there. What happened to all his followers? He had to feel very alone at this point. The man hanging (referred to as the "good thief") beside him understood who Jesus was and was forgiven. In the garden, when Jesus was arrested, they all forsook Him and fled! Can you imagine the rejection and hurt that he must have felt that even his closest friends left him?

How many of us would have done the same thing?

When we look at Peter, we are, in effect, all Peters, aren't we?

In the Garden of Gethsemane, Peter's anger caused him to cut off the ear of the servant of the high priest.

Peter denied Jesus three times.

Peter also did miracles, and he cast out demons.

Peter also knew who Jesus was and said, "You are the Christ, the son of the living God." Yet his courage seemed to come and go.

⚓ Notes: ⚓

For Further Examination

In Acts, Peter was filled again with courage. He was threatened and ordered to stop preaching. He continued witnessing.

Peter was able to perform miracles. He told the cripple person to get up and walk, and he did.

He proclaimed to all I have come to tell you about Jesus Christ whom you have crucified.

The Holy Spirit is what made the difference with Peter, and his presence will make the difference with us also.

We should not be too hard on the disciples; after all, many of us have done the same by our sin. What happened to Peter can indeed happen to us.

Jesus transformed the disciples and also many people's lives. If he did this for them, he will also transform our lives. We need to express daily our gratitude for all God has done for us. We need to see ourselves from God's perspective. I always say God must have a great sense of humor to put up with a person like me. We should compare ourselves only to God and not to anyone else. This comparison will open our eyes to areas that we need to work on. Follow the prompting of the Holy Spirit and do what he instructs.

Can you just imagine what this world would be like if all were followers of God? Learn to disciple others and we will all be followers of God. Let us start being the hands and feet of Jesus!

◄ Notes: ►

About The Author

Larry is a PK (preacher's kid) and was originally from Canada. He moved to Riley Center, MI, when he was five. Growing up in the church, he learned that we are all hypocrites and sinners and left the church. Eventually, he returned and went on to complete his ministry degree. In addition to being known professionally as "Larry the Computer Guy" (through his IT company,) he also runs a non-denominational Christian retreat center on his 17-acre ranch.

Footnotes and References:

Peter

Bibliography F. Josephus, Antiquities of the Jews (95), XX. 9, 1, 2; J. Lightfoot, The Epistle of Paul to the Galatians (1865), 252-291; A. Plummer, The General Epistles of St. James and St. Jude (1891), 25-41; C. Weizsäcker, The Apostolic Age of the Christian Church (1894), 196-198; G. Purves, Christianity in the Apostolic Age (1900), 130-150; J. Mayor, The Epistle of St. James (1913), i-lxv; M. James, The Apocryphal New Testament (1926), 3, 4; F. Filson, Pioneers of the Primitive Church (1940), 155-183; A. Ross, The Epistles of James and John (1954), 12-17; R. Tasker. The General Epistle of James (1957), 22-30; A. Smith, The Twelve Christ Chose (1958), 33-48, 109-118; W. Barclay, The Master's Men (1959), 82-86, 100-104; E. Bishop, "Mary (of) Clopas and Her Father" ETh 73/11 (1962), 339.

John

Bibliography F. Josephus, Antiquities of the Jews (95), XX. 9, 1, 2; J. Lightfoot, The Epistle of Paul to the Galatians (1865), 252-291; A. Plummer, The General Epistles of St. James and St. Jude (1891), 25-41; C. Weizsäcker, The Apostolic Age of the Christian Church (1894), 196-198; G. Purves, Christianity in the Apostolic Age (1900), 130-150; J. Mayor, The Epistle of St. James (1913), i-lxv; M. James, The Apocryphal New Testament (1926), 3, 4; F. Filson, Pioneers of the Primitive Church (1940), 155-183; A. Ross, The Epistles of James and John (1954), 12-17; R. Tasker. The General Epistle of James (1957), 22-30; A. Smith, The Twelve Christ Chose (1958), 33-48, 109-118; W. Barclay, The Master's Men (1959), 82-86, 100-104; E. Bishop, "Mary (of) Clopas and Her Father" ETh 73/11 (1962), 339.

James

Bibliography M. R. James, The Apocryphal New Testament (1924), 337-363, 453-460, 472-475; G. Dalman, Sacred Sites and Ways (Eng. tr., 1935), 161-163; F. Dvornik, The Idea of Apostolicity in Byzantium and the Legend of the Apostle Andrew (1958); P. M. Peterson, Andrew, Brother of Simon Peter—His History and His Legends (1958); W. Barclay, The Master's Men (1959), 40-46.

Philip

Bibliography W. M. Ramsay, Cities and Bishoprics of Phrygia, I (1895-1897), ii, 552; B. P. Grenfell and A. B. Hunt (eds.), The Hibeh Papyri, I (1906), 62. 1; M. R. James, The Apocryphal NT (1924), 439-453.

Bibliography J. Hastings, The Greater Men and Women of the Bible, Vol. VI (1916), 115-134.

Bartholomew

Bibliography M. R. James, The Apocryphal NT (1924), 166-186; 467, 468; D. Browne, "Who Was Nathanael?" ExpT, XXXVIII (1927), 286; R. B. Y. Scott, "Who Was Nathanael?" ExpT XXXVIII (1927), 93, 94; W. P. Barker, Twelve Who Were Chosen (1957), 57-63; W. Barclay, The Master's Men (1959), 102-113.

Matthew

Bibliography A. Fahling, *The Life of Christ* (1936); M. C. Tenney, *The New Testament: An Historical And Analytic Survey* (1954), 151-164; M. Franzmann, *Follow Me: Discipleship According To Saint Matthew* (1961), 1-33; M. H. Franzmann, *The Word of The Lord Grows* (1961); *The Interpreter's Bible*, Vol. 7, D. Guthrie, *New Testament Introduction: The Gospel and Acts* (1965), 19-48.

Thaddaeus

Bibliography H. B. Swete, *The Gospel According to St. Mark* (1905), 61; V. Taylor, *The Gospel According to St. Mark* (1952), 233, 234.

Simon the Zealot

Bibliography "Simonians," J. H. Blunt, ed., Dictionary of Sects, Heresies, Ecclesiastical Parties, and Schools of Religious Thought (1874); R. M. Grant, Gnosticism and Early Christianity (1960), ch. 3.

Judas Iscariot

Bibliography E. F. Harrison, "Jesus and Judas," *Bibliotheca Sacra* 417 (Jan-March 1948), 170-181; F. J. Foakes-Jackson and Kirsopp Lake, "The Death of Judas," in F. J. Foakes-Jackson and K. Lake, *The Beginnings of Christianity*, Vol. V (1933), 22-30. For an exhaustive treatment, consult J. G. Tasker, "Judas Iscariot," in Hastings DCG, I, pp. 907-913 (1906).

Other Inspiration

https://www.crosswalk.com/church/pastors-or-leadership/ask-roger/how-the-disciples-failures-give-us-hope-for-today.html

Made in the USA
Monee, IL
01 December 2021

83595750R00068